Reading Roundabout

I am a Christian

James Nixon

Photography by Chris Fairclough

W

First published in 2007 by
Franklin Watts
338 Euston Road
London NW1 3BH

Franklin Watts Australia
Level 17/207 Kent Street
Sydney NSW 2000

ISBN: 978 0 7496 7445 8 (hbk)
ISBN: 978 0 7496 7457 1 (pbk)

Dewey classification number: 230

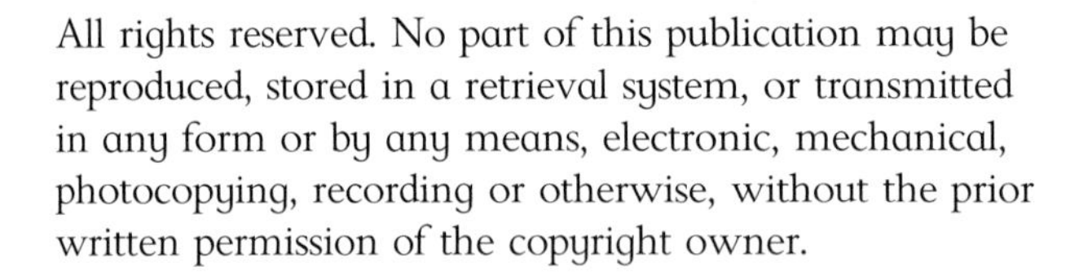

A CIP catalogue record for this book is available from the British Library.

Planning and production by Discovery Books Limited
Editor: James Nixon
Designer: Ian Winton
Photography: Chris Fairclough
Series advisors: Diana Bentley MA and Dee Reid MA,
Fellows of Oxford Brookes University

The author, packager and publisher would like to thank the following people for their participation in this book: Louis and Lizzie Smith and family; St. Mary Magdelene Church, Eardisley, Herefordshire.

All photographs by Chris Fairclough except for p. 19: Jill Fromer/istockphoto.com.

Printed in China

Franklin Watts is a division of Hachette Children's books, an Hachette Livre UK company.

Contents

I am a Christian

My name is Louis
and I am a Christian.

Christians believe in God and his son Jesus Christ.

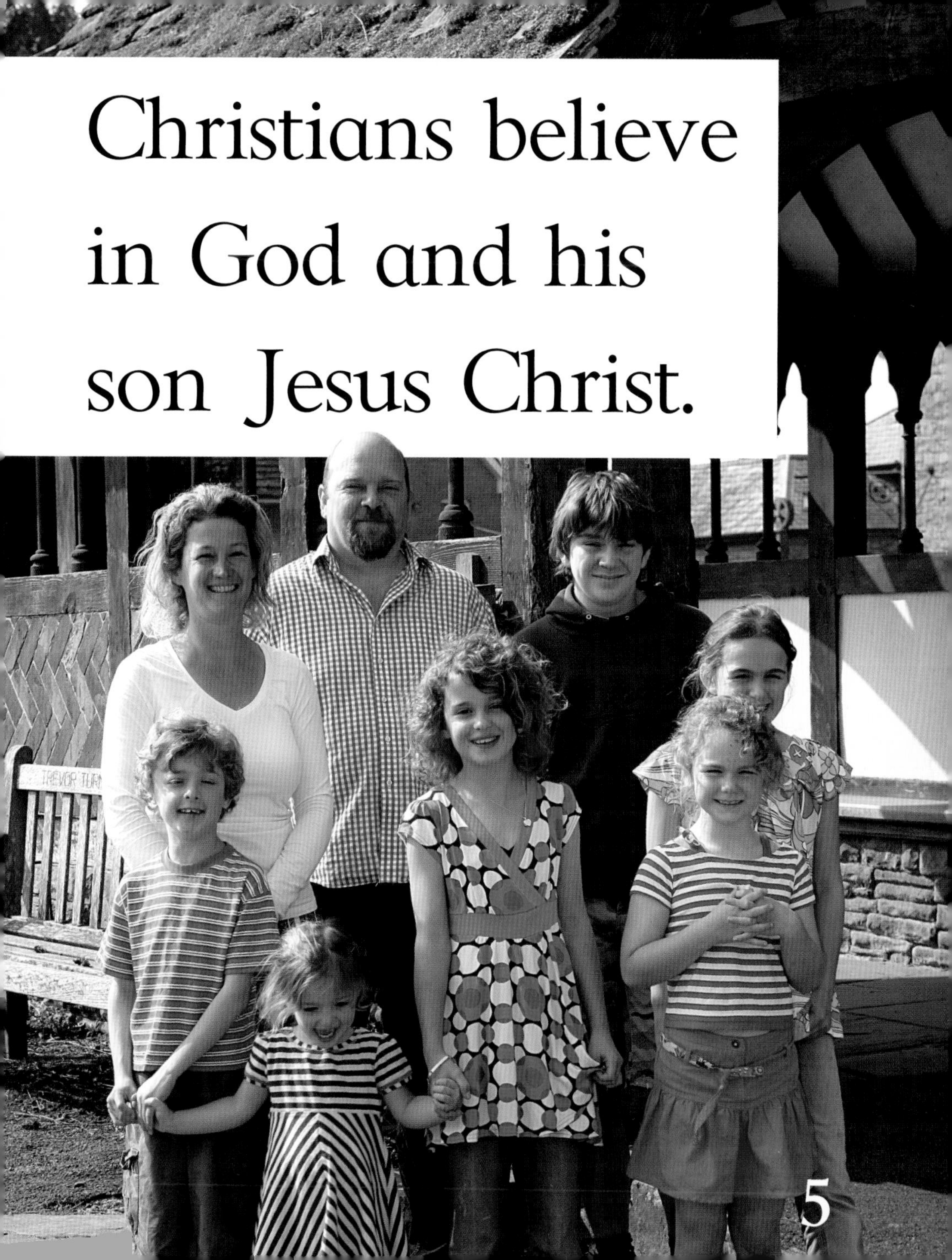

Going to church

On a Sunday we go to church...

...to worship God together.

Praising God

Christians show their love for God in many ways.

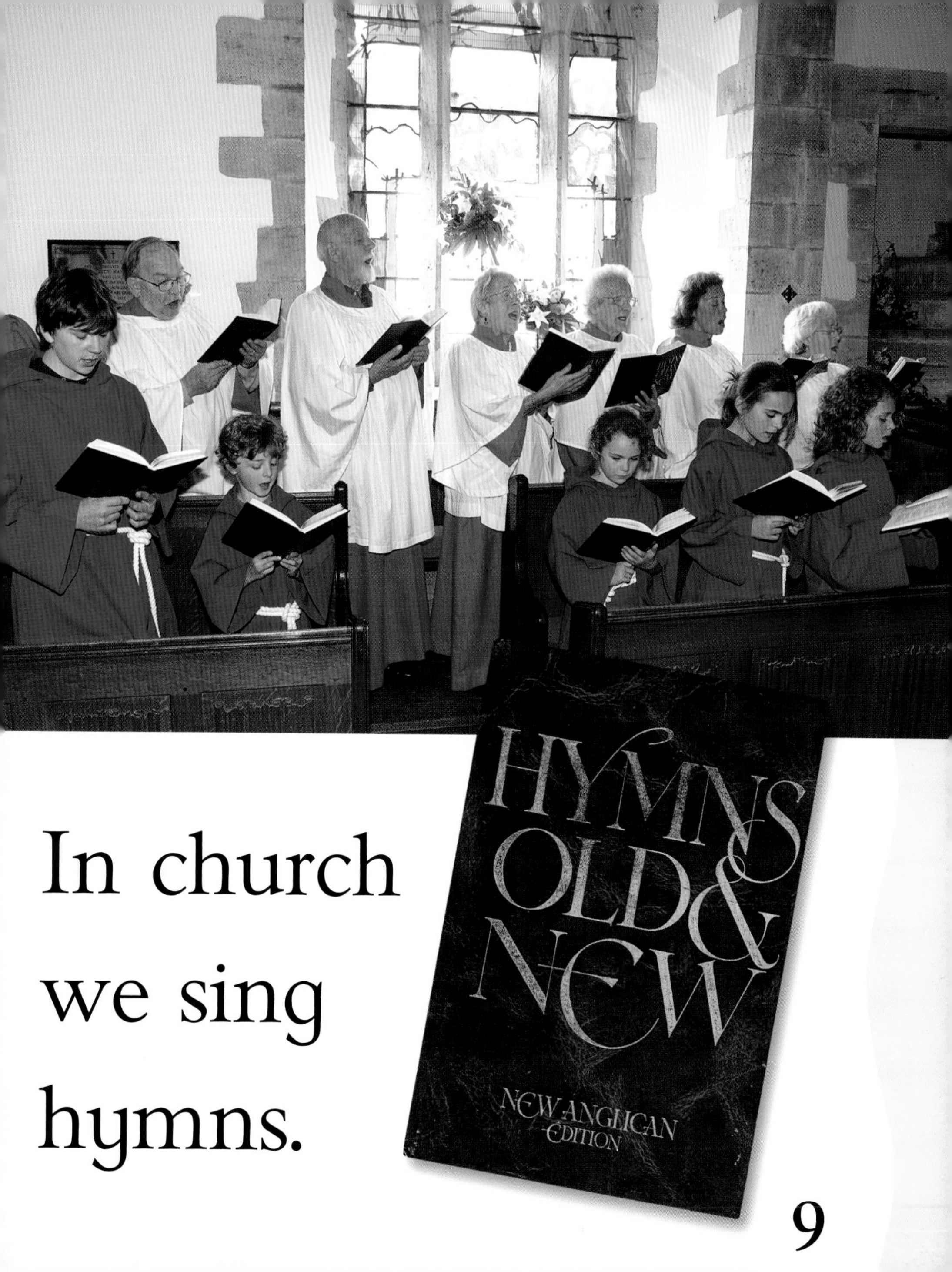

In church we sing hymns.

Praying to God

When I pray
I thank God for
the good things.

Sometimes I ask
God for his help.

Reading the Bible

We believe the Bible is the word of God.

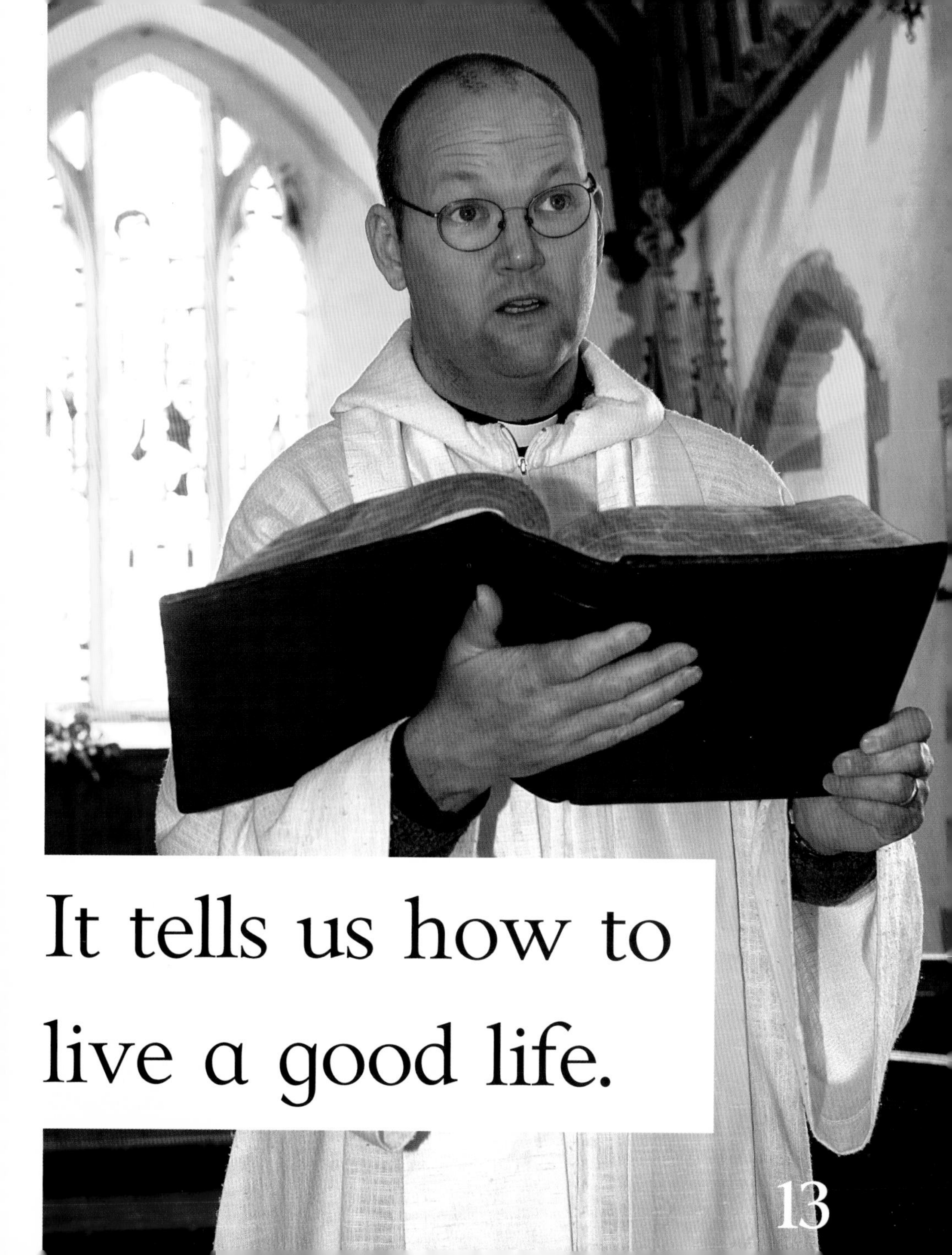

It tells us how to live a good life.

Learning about Jesus

In Sunday school we learn about Jesus.

The Bible tells us how Jesus lived.

Helping others

Jesus taught us to love everybody.

He taught us to help the poor.

Festivals

Christians have many festivals.

At Christmas we celebrate the birth of Jesus.

Easter time

At Easter we celebrate Jesus rising from the dead...

...and new life.

Jesus loves me

I am happy being a Christian.

I know Jesus loves me.

Word bank

Look back for these words and pictures.

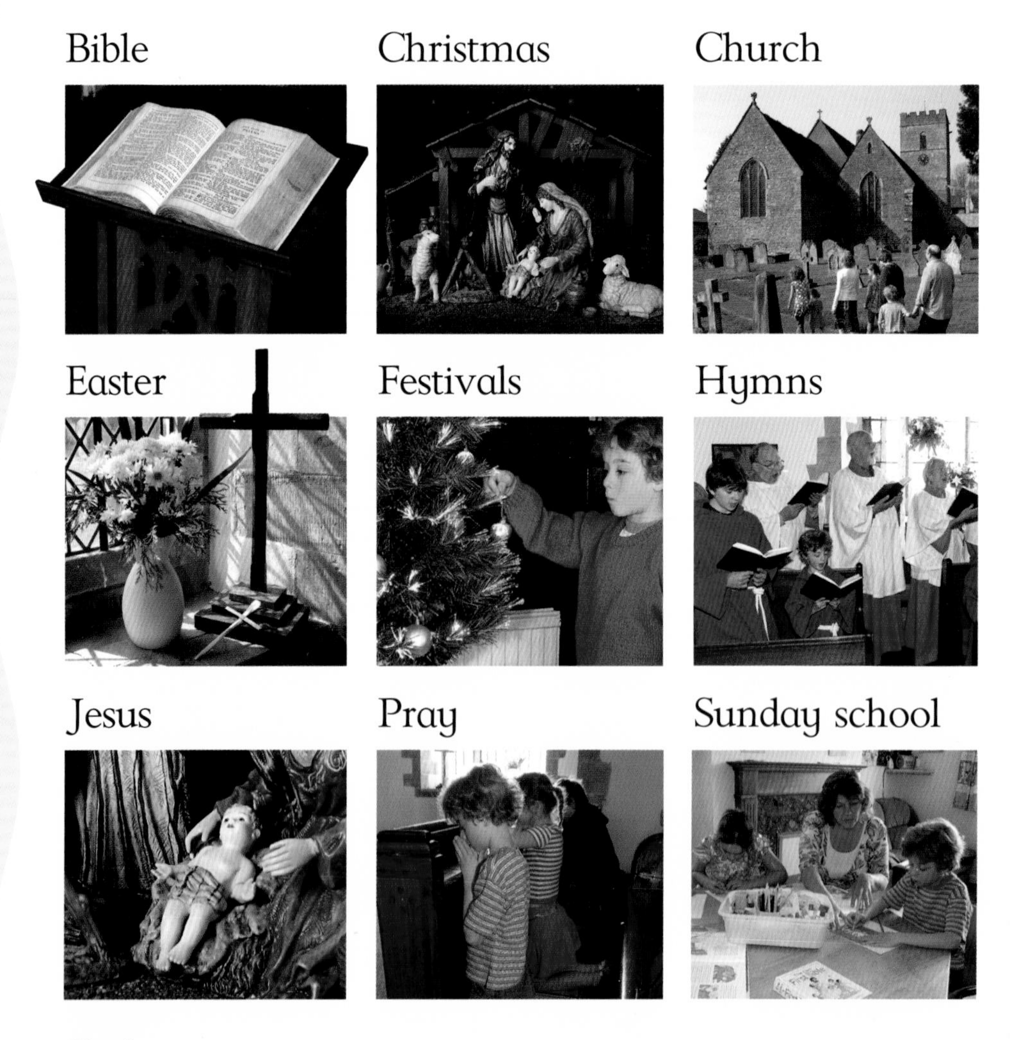

Bible

Christmas

Church

Easter

Festivals

Hymns

Jesus

Pray

Sunday school